FOREVER 27

FOREVER

SELENA WILLIAMS

PALMETTO
PUBLISHING

Charleston, SC
www.PalmettoPublishing.com

Forever 27
Copyright © 2021 by Selena Williams

First Edition

ISBN: 978-1-63837-838-9

TABLE OF CONTENTS

Intro   vii

1. Growing Up   1

2. The Truth   13

3. Broken Family   19

4. Hope   26

5. Faith   33

6. Black Heart   48

7. Facing Reality   58

8. Forever Demons   74

9. Honor   88

About the Author   103

INTRO

A day that forever changed our lives...

You suddenly feel entirely numb inside from a single phone call that you prayed every day for years that you would never receive. Why was someone so amazing taken away from life way too young? Why couldn't he fight these demons any longer? Why are people so judgmental about mental illness? These are questions I ask myself every single day since a horrible nightmare came true so suddenly, and now I have to face the demons added forever onto who I am now. Continuing to wake up, seeing the sunrise, and knowing that reality continues with my brother being gone is a slap in the face. There's a massive difference between someone being sick and "being a bad person" that, sadly, people quickly opinionate on about mental illness. Still, truthfully, they're not educated enough about the subject.

In honor of my older brother, Jacob, a demon inside of him that he could no longer shake.

"May the wind always be at your back and the sun upon your face, and may the wings of destiny carry you aloft to dance with the stars."

—*Blow*

1

GROWING UP

Growing up, we didn't have a white picket fence, but we had a great mom and such a great life and a childhood I will forever be grateful for having. It was always the three of us, and people called us "The Three Musketeers." Our mom worked as hard as she could to make sure Jacob and I were always taken care of, always provided for, and got us whatever we wanted or needed for holidays, birthdays, or any sport we desired to play. She made sure we were signed up and had anything necessary to play. You would've never thought our mom struggled with finances behind closed doors as a single parent. Our mom was beyond proud of Jacob and me and constantly reminded us every single day to make sure we knew and felt how loved we truly were by her. Every good grade, spelling test, report card, she ensured to take the time and celebrate the success.

Jacob and I were just like any other children. We went through the phases of games, hobbies, only wanting name-brand clothes, and the normal puberty phases of growing up into wild teenagers. Mom always did special things for us, and to this day, I'll never forget them—roller skating, club kids, going to the Dairy Queen and getting a dilly bar. I remember Jacob and I would be so still and silent, trying not to have ants in our pants in the back seat and goof off with each other because we knew Mom was getting closer to the Dairy Queen, and if we weren't on our best behavior, we weren't getting a treat. It was always the smallest things that meant so much to Jacob and me, like being beyond happy to go to the grocery store with Mom and being able to pick out a Kid's Cuisine frozen dinner or getting a Happy Meal from McDonald's because I thought the box was cool. Jacob cared about switching toys that came in them. Jacob used to laugh so hard when Mom would take us to Walmart and I would cry when I saw the live lobsters in the tank.

My mom did whatever it took, even if it meant working longer hours to make sure we always got our needs or wants. We were great and happy kids. She even took us to work when it was kids' day. I remember we loved going and pretending to be an adult like our mom with our own name badges she had made for us. While Mom worked, we spent time at our grandparents' house, and every single summer break, we went there as well, along with our cousins. We had the best memories, loving every bit of being spoiled, playing games like four square, just running around outside, racing bikes, and playing basketball with a game called Horse. We were taught how to ride our bikes, make mud pies outside, and we would always use our imaginations to create fun games. We walked into town to get ice cream and loved getting our "family tradition" sugar popcorn, that our grandfather always made for us. I will be forever grateful for such heartfelt memories of everyone being together.

Jacob and I did everything together; we were practically joined at the hip. I looked up to my big brother so much, and I wanted to always follow in his footsteps. He was protective; he was always so proud of me and always needed my help when it came to helping him win a game or trying the newest wrestling move out on me that he had learned at wrestling practice. If you asked Jacob who I was, he would always reply with "my sissy." He never wanted his friends to say I was cute or even for them to play with me since he was always such a protective and caring older brother.

Jacob and I had the same father as well. He was my only full-blood sibling, and that's why our bond was unexplainable. Our dad and mom split when Jacob and I were very young, I wasn't even a year old. At the time, my mom and dad were young parents, and sadly my dad just didn't have it in him to have the passion for taking care of Jacob and me. My mom played both roles, and even though my dad wasn't around very often, she always allowed my dad to be in the picture and wanted him to be around. He would see us on his terms; he would come to my brother's baseball games. When we went over to our dad's house, I wouldn't leave Jacob's side. He and I would ask my dad for some change, and Jacob and I would walk down to the police station on my dad's road because the station had a soda machine outside of it. Jacob and I would play with my Easy-Bake Oven and play hide-and-seek around the house at night. Dad would turn the lights off, and we would love playing a couple of rounds. We would also have campouts in the living room at bedtime; we would watch cartoons together until we fell asleep.

In the summertime, Dad, Jacob, and I walked to the pool, and we could go play on the playground at the school near my dad's house. I don't remember a lot of childhood with my dad, but I do remember some great memories being with Jacob there because I was a mommy's brat. I never liked being away from my mom for a long time, so I was happy to always have my brother with me. My brother acted just like my father, and I was my mom's "twin" through and through. My father then had our little sister a few years later, and then in 2020, he had our second little sister.

In 2004, our mom got married to our stepdad. He already had two girls of his own, so having stepsisters was something new for me and was a big adjustment to our life. I was used to having my own toys, my own room, and my own space, and that all changed quickly. We became a big blended family in such a small house, but we made it work. My mom and stepdad then had our little brother.

We were raised to be active and always be outside rather than sitting in the house. We always had two options: help Mom clean the house all day or play outside. We always chose outside. Nothing was ever perfect, but us four kids being all around the same age made things an adventure; we had the biggest laughs and memories in that small house. We would play manhunt, go swimming, and, of course, make a whirlpool or dunk each other; we would get on the four-wheelers and try to get the back person to catch some air as we went over tall hills that we made in the fields, and we always played and made up games. We were so competitive; on the field, we would play baseball, soccer, and even freeze tag. We made our own rules. We had a trampoline that I always "took over" because I was a cheerleader. I always wanted to work on my flips and cheer routines. We would collect ladybugs and worms. In the summer, we were so wild and reckless when our parents brought out the Slip N' Slide. We would sprint, slide, and skid our bodies across the grass, but we never minded because we were too busy having a blast together. At night, we ran around barefoot, collecting lightening bugs in a mason jar and would set the tent up out back. We always swore we were going to sleep in the tent all night, that never happened because I would get scared of noises. But, when Jacob had friends over they would camp outside. I loved sneaking around the side of the house to try and scare them. It never worked, Jacob always said, "it's boy time only." Us five kids would all hang out in my bedroom at night time, watching scary movies and looking up funny videos on the internet. We jammed out to the radio and always found something to have fun altogether, even if it would get us into trouble sometimes, because pranks got a little wild.

As a family, we always went camping. We went from sleeping in tents to having a camper. Still, the memories of growing up camping in those tiny tents are the memories I will cherish forever. I will never forget the time my bumblebee tent flooded one camping trip when there was a huge storm. It is a memory our family looks back on can always laugh about today. Getting on the bikes and riding on the trails to hide from our parents, getting on teams and playing manhunt at the campgrounds, going to the beaches and trying to catch the tallest wave we could go under because we would compete against each other to see who would be too scared. Climbing up the towers at cape, trying to go as fast as we could on the big hill, and the late nights playing UNO at the family table by the fire and enjoying a nice s'more afterward. Looking back now, those times together as a family will forever stay close to my heart. Knowing my brother and I had some of the best memories together and knowing we will never get that opportunity again makes the memories even more meaningful.

My dad would take us to Cherrystone, and we would fish all weekend on the boat, play mini golf, and drive the golf cart at the latest hours of the night playing manhunt because Jacob would be on a ground bike hiding somewhere. We played in the arcade, and Jacob would tell me to put my arm up the claw machine to try and grab stuffed animals for free. We would use the paddleboats until our legs were exhausted, and we would play water war with other kids at the campground, battling over and over until we won every game.

On weekends after a long school week, we went ice skating which was the best because we hid so many secrets from our parents and were able to flirt with people. We had such great memories and nights that, at the time, felt like we were on cloud nine with our crushes, thinking that holding hands on the ice meant we were getting married.

Jacob and I grew up with a family who also had a daughter and son about the same age as Jacob and I, and that family basically became our family. The four of us were together all the time; they were the closest two people Jacob and I ever had as friends. Being older now and understanding more about life, I know our parents didn't have all kinds of money back in the day when we were younger, but they never let us kids know that. We never went without something, and we always received anything for birthdays or Christmas that we wished to have. I loved going through magazines and circling toys with Jacob, and we were truly blessed and so spoiled, not even realizing it.

We loved our lives, and especially school because it came pretty easy to Jacob and me. We had numerous friends, and we were strong athletes. Jacob was an absolute star; in high school, he played varsity soccer, wrestling, and baseball, and he was the captain for his teams for years. He was popular and beyond smart, so grades were a breeze. I entered high school two years later, and being Jacob's sister made school so easy because Jacob was so well known. I had a great advantage in being his younger sister. Going into my classes for the new school year, my new teachers used to ask, "Are you Jacob's sister?" When I said yes, the response was always the best. They would say, "Oh boy, I hope you're not as wild as your brother." Of course, I was.

Jacob didn't like when I talked to him in the hallway, though. He acted too cool for me! It was okay. I yelled "I love you, brother!" every time I saw him, and I would give him a huge hug just to pluck his nerves. One day in the hallway, I went up to give Jacob a huge hug in front of his friends, so he decided to pick me up over his shoulder and he put me into the yellow trashcan. Yes, it was empty. It was so hilarious. At times, I would be in class and Jacob would text me saying I needed to meet him at a certain area in the school. He would need me to record him doing something, and other times it would be something as simple as change for a soda. I came every single time he needed me. I rode with Jacob to school sometimes, he didn't care for it. I would get dressed slower or wake up late to miss the bus on purpose, so that I could ride in Jacob's car. I thought it was cool rolling into school with my big brother. I soon dated Jacob's best friend, and he continually dated my friends, so we were always together hanging out. Jacob and I became stronger best friends the older we became, going to parties, sneaking out, hiding secrets only he and I knew. Life was a blast; we were young and crazy.

Jacob also started playing adult softball. Those night games and weekend games were seriously some of the best times I ever spent with my brother. His girlfriend at the time and I would go and watch to support our boyfriends. It was so nice that my brother's girlfriends and I always got along as best friends. But suddenly, one of my brother's best friends who he wrestled with passed away due to suicide, and it crushed my brother. He started hanging out with people who weren't leaders. Instead, what they were did in their eyes at the time meant they were "cool." Jacob started becoming more of the class clown, doing small, immature things that would get him into trouble. At the time, it didn't seem like a huge problem because every teenager goes through that "trouble" phase in their own way.

As time went on, my brother was kicked out of high school. He then started adult education to finish his schooling, but that came to an end as well. My dad and Jacob started butting heads with each other more and more as time went on. They didn't see eye to eye on a lot of things and what Jacob was doing in life, and when it came to arguing, it only escalated with time. One night, we were at a party with my dad, and Jacob and our dad got into an actual fistfight. Of course, I tried getting into the middle of the fight to protect my brother, but my dad pushed me, making Jacob so mad that he went off immediately. Jacob always stood up for me, and I remember I had to call my mom and stepdad to hurry and get there because the entire situation was becoming worse. I saw blood in the driveway, and my little sister was screaming, crying, and gripping onto me. It was disgusting.

From that night forward, Jacob and my dad went through a rocky relationship with each other, the same with my dad and me. I had nothing to say to my dad for a while, and I couldn't understand how he could put his hands like that on his own child. But, if anyone knew the relationship between Jacob and my dad, they knew my dad could do anything to Jacob. Jacob would forgive him like nothing ever happened because they both acted the exact same way, literally—the way they acted and talked, anger issues, and overall who they were. My mom could tell you the trouble Jacob was getting into; our dad had acted the same way growing up. They were "bad boys."

As I struggled to figure out what was going on with my brother, Jacob made a promise to our grandfather to finish high school, and he made that promise come true. Jacob finished high school online and walked at a ceremony to receive his diploma. We were so proud of Jacob for finishing something he had promised to do; it was such a beautiful moment watching him walk, and we had so much hope that this day meant Jacob had a big and bright future ahead of him. We knew Jacob was smart and bright enough to do whatever he desired to do in life. But there has to come a time in your own mind that it's time to gear up, to start making adult decisions for yourself to make a great life. Being a troubled teenager fades away the older you become; maturity changes and hopefully help teaches you to grow up, but at least we thought it did.

2

THE TRUTH

Jacob was very popular. Being popular comes with different types of baggage, sometimes good and sometimes terrible. Being at parties, seeing things that the "cool kids" are doing, on top of dealing with normal puberty and hormones, comes with a lot of questions. You become very curious. Still, I always saw just teenage normal stupid things like cigarettes or alcohol. Teenagers think doing stuff like that at parties makes you cool and not a wussy. Trust me, I know because I went through the phase, and I did it; I was no saint. So seeing Jacob other than normal wasn't possible because

I knew we were wild kids; we just loved partying on and having a good time.

In your life, there has always to come a time where you ask yourself, "Are you a leader, or are you becoming a follower? My brother started falling through the cracks slowly, day by day, and none of us saw it coming because it wasn't something we ever thought we would have to pay attention to, nor did we think our family would go through something so serious. Jacob and I were normal teenagers; we got into a little bit of trouble, we were grounded at times, and we ran our mouths a little more than we should have, but what teenager is perfect?

It was Christmas Eve; my little brother and I were in the kitchen baking cookies, and our mom said, "Where's Jacob? We're making his favorite cookies. He should come out here and help."

Mom walked down the hallway to Jacob's room and immediately shut the door behind her. Mom was in the bedroom for a little while and then suddenly walked out of the bedroom. She came back into the kitchen. I noticed she had been crying and that Jacob never came out of his bedroom, so I suddenly asked, "Mom, is everything okay?"

She quickly answered, "Yes, everything's fine. Jacob just isn't feeling well."

I didn't think anything of it; I figured Jacob was just sick like my mom said and that, hopefully, he would be better by tomorrow morning since it was Christmas. On Christmas day every year, we always spent the entire Christmas day together, just me and him going from our mom's side of the family to my dad's house. I always looked forward to that day. So the next day, we all woke up as a family, opened gifts, and everything was great like always. I asked Jacob if he was feeling okay, and he just told me that his stomach had hurt the night before, but he was fine. I was happy because it was our day together.

I looked up to Jacob so much and always felt so much closer in our sibling bond every time we spent time together. He would take the time just to spend time with his sissy, and he would be so nice to me, wanting to take sibling pictures. He actually would post the pictures on his social media, saying that he loved his sissy. It truly meant so much to me because what teenage boy would want to hang out with his sister? Not many, so it was so nice to spend all day together. We would get ready after opening gifts and having breakfast at Mom's, get a coffee, and then go to our dad's. I had always cherished Christmas because I loved riding with Jacob. I felt cool being in his passenger seat with his music booming and the seats vibrating. It was a perfect day with our family, spending time together and just enjoying the holiday just like any other year.

In his car, Jacob and I always talked about life. We shared everything with each other, so I always knew all of Jacob's secrets, good or bad. We were literally best friends. We helped each other through a lot of trouble and certain things only Jacob and I knew about. I knew Jacob would always have my back—be my ride or die—and I knew Jacob was just a rowdy teenager who thought about parties, young fun, and girls every chance he got. But several days after Christmas, my mom came upstairs to my bedroom, shut the door behind her, and said, "Selena, I need to talk to you about something." Tears started flowing down her face as she told me I needed to listen and just understand what she was about to say. She then told me that on Christmas Eve when she walked into Jacob's bedroom, Jacob had been sitting on his bed with a needle. She had no idea what he was doing; in fact, she had to look it up because she knew nothing about drugs or what it had even looked like. She didn't know what to think of the situation. I was a teenage girl at the time, so my initial reaction was "Okay, Mom, he will be fine." I had zero knowledge about heroin or any drug in general, so I didn't put any thought into it.

Weeks went by, and even months went by, and then I started seeing unusual things. I was young and wild, so I would be out late at night. I would come home, and cars I had never seen before would be in the driveway. Jacob would be sitting out in them. Jacob would ask me to take him here and there, he would ask me for money, but I still didn't put much thought into it because I honestly wasn't educated enough about addiction. I didn't look at Jacob in any other way than "that's my big brother." I felt cool every time Jacob needed me because a lot of brothers don't pay attention to their sisters when they're teenagers. I also never saw Jacob looking physically any different, and his personality to me seemed the exact same.

Then one day, I was at my friend's house when my mom called me and said, "You need to come home for a little while to talk with the entire family." So I left, pulled into the driveway, and walked inside. My mom, stepdad, and Jacob were all sitting on the couch. Instantly, my heart sank; I knew something was wrong. As we sat there, my parents explained how severe Jacob's addiction had become in full detail. As I started to cry, my mom said, "Jacob, do you see how hurt your sister is? She loves you, we love you, what do you need from us to stop this? We cannot continue down this path. This has to stop."

On the couch, Jacob looked at me and said, "I'm sorry, sis." He said he would stop. I believed him; we all believed him. But if you know anything about addiction, it's not that easy. Sadly, we didn't know much about addiction at that time or how quickly things could get worse. We didn't know how Jacob truly felt. At the time, we weren't educated to get a grip on the problem quickly enough to get him some help and fast solutions such as rehab to get Jacob out of that mess. But, yet again, we didn't expect this in our worst dreams. Honestly, we didn't think Jacob would continue down this dark path of life. We thought Jacob, being the great person we always knew he was, strong and crazy smart, would overcome this. On top of having the family sit-down conversation we had together and seeing how hurt we all were, we truly thought it would help Jacob and change his views and decisions about continuing to do this to himself. Who would ever think their family was about to go through actual hell and face demons larger than we ever imagined? We surely didn't. Furthermore, if you told me my brother would fight and suffer from this deadly disease for nine years, I would've called you insane.

3

BROKEN FAMILY

I was young, and I said numerous things that I regret and wish I could take back. My mom was broken, but I was very selfish, and I regret it every single day. I didn't understand back then, and I didn't realize the reality of what happens to someone with an addiction to drugs. I didn't realize how it affected my mom because I'm not a parent. She hid a lot of how she was feeling inside.

Everyone took the truth and handled it differently. We thought it was a phase and that Jacob would overcome it. I said a lot of stupid things to my mom instead of supporting her as I should have. Do you know how it feels as a parent to constantly keep waking up because you hear something odd, walk downstairs, and see your child selling things from the house to get a drug? How it feels to never sleep because you're afraid to walk downstairs, not knowing if your child is alive or not? Having to walk around and constantly watch everything. Any sign, any noise or anything that may seem strange. It's absolutely beyond horrible, and it hurt my mom and stepdad so much. They knew Jacob wasn't doing it for the hell of it; it was because drugs were literally taking over his brain. He didn't want to hurt my parents, but he could only think about one thing at the time, and at that time, my brother only wanted his demons silenced. He didn't want to do drugs. Unfortunately, a drug was the only solution that made him feel any different, and many people don't understand that. But I said the worst comments to her like "How about you worry about your son doing drugs and not what I'm doing" or "Oh yeah, poor Jacob." I hold regret inside of me for that, and it will be something I have to carry as a demon forever. It continued with me acting like a selfish brat, and my mom broke apart, crying and yelling at me to shut up and to please stop as tears rolled down her face.

What's so disgusting is that I didn't react. I was too worried about putting my makeup on to get ready to go out and party all night. Now reflecting on my past, I know why I partied so much, though. I know why I drank so much. I was upset about Jacob. I was so sad that my brother was going through something so awful. I took out my anger and sadness through drinking so that I wouldn't feel the pain I had inside. I remember getting drunk so many times when I shouldn't have, and I would cry so much. I would let out everything that I was feeling and explain what my family was struggling through. People didn't understand, though. They didn't live in it like my family and I did. I was never rude to Jacob, so sadly, I just took out how I was feeling on my mom, and I should've never done that.

My dad had given up on my brother completely—constant fistfights, calling the cops on my brother. It was stupid. My dad said ignorant comments all the time like "Your mom is a better person than me" and "Why does she deal with his bullshit when she doesn't have to? He's a grown-ass man and needs to learn." My mom always mentioned that the Williams family couldn't be around each other when we were all drinking, and she was absolutely right. Every time alcohol was involved and we were drinking at my dad's house, severe anger would come out of all three of us, and the outcome was never pretty.

One day, my dad found out Jacob had written a check out in his checkbook and called the cops on my brother. My mom called me at work and told me to get home quickly. When I got home, Jacob was sitting on the couch with a bag in between his legs and his head down, crying and saying he messed up. Instead of my dad seeing that Jacob was struggling and realizing his son needed his help, he just wanted my brother locked up. He said the worst things to his face, called him a junkie and anything else you could think of. I didn't get it.

With my mom being the parent she was to us, she wouldn't allow something bad to happen to Jacob. So my mom had me quickly drive to the nearest bank and get money out of her account for what my brother had taken from my dad so that nothing would happen to him. I pulled back into my mom's driveway with money, and moments later, my dad pulled up, screaming his ass off. He pointed his finger at my mom's house, yelling, "Tell my piece of shit son to come outside." It was devastating. I screamed, sticking up for my brother as always, telling my dad just to leave.

My dad didn't allow Jacob to stay at his house even for a single night to give my mom a break—not a damn thing. It was awful to see Jacob hurting so much. He loved my dad beyond words, and all he wanted was for my dad to accept him for who he was. My dad didn't, not even once.

Time went on, and I started seeing more signs of my brother falling apart. Certain things were missing from the house all the time. My mom was putting things up so that Jacob couldn't find them. My mom made sure I brought my wallet inside from my car every day. Jacob took random walks down the road at the most unusual times, and making sure money was never out in the open was just the start of this nightmare. The entire household felt on edge 24-7, and it only got worse.

I tried to tell Mom about the random vehicles I saw late at night coming home and anything else I saw that I felt like she needed to know. But the response was always pretty bitter: "Don't have money in your bedroom" or "Tell your brother no when he asks you to take him somewhere you know she shouldn't be at, Selena." She was absolutely right, but when you're young, you never think about the consequences of going to drug meets, sketchy houses, or the most random areas. I didn't want to think that my brother was actually doing drugs, so I just denied the truth in my own mind. Mom was right; I shouldn't have had money out—I knew that—but it was me having to change so many normal habits that I struggled with the worst. But even more so, I could never tell Jacob no. I just didn't know how to because I still looked up to Jacob as my amazing, great brother because he was so amazing. But I knew I didn't know how to help him.

Months went by, nothing felt any different, but I still didn't put a lot of thought into the situation because Jacob still looked fine in my eyes. Then, one night I went out to my friends' house because they were having people over. I randomly received a text message from my mom, and she told me again that I needed to come home for the night. Once I got home, my mom and I sat upstairs talking about Jacob. My mom explained to me that Jacob was getting worse, he was becoming sicker, and that we needed to work as a family to figure out how we were going to help Jacob. That night, I sat in my bedroom wondering what the hell was going on. As I researched signs and reactions to using heroin on my phone, it was overwhelming. The pictures were devastating.

The following week, I was at a friend's party when my mom called my phone and asked, "Selena, have you had anything to drink?"

I answered back, saying a glass of wine or two. She quickly responded with "Give your friend your phone."

I did. My friend talked to my mom for a minute and then gave me back the phone with my mom saying, "Selena, do not leave that house. Jacob just overdosed, and I'm on my way to him right now. I will inform you when I get home."

I knew what an overdose meant. Still, I didn't understand how severe and scary it actually was. My heart just sank, and I started crying. I stayed at my friend's house for a little longer, but I couldn't get my thoughts straight, so I headed home. Once I got home, my mom pulled in soon after, and she sat me down and told me what happened. My brother was in the hospital, and it broke me. I knew right at that moment I needed to be around more, to be present and support my mom more. I also needed to start learning and understanding what addiction truly was and what I could do to help my brother in any way possible. I started seeing changes in my mom's marriage—struggling, arguments, and a lot of crying behind closed doors. Our family was falling apart, and I didn't know what to do. Time went forward, and I knew I needed to change my life around. I needed to grow up, and I knew I needed to step up and help my family.

4

HOPE

It was time to help and support Jacob so he knew he wasn't struggling alone. We were there to uplift him and to give him nothing but love and a positive mind-set. We started putting emotions to the side and truly focusing on helping Jacob get better. He went through phases of up and down changes with his health. Jacob was still always there for me. I still went out to parties, and when I didn't want to call my mom to get me at the late hours of the night, I would call Jacob. He and his friends would be right there to rescue my best friend and me so I didn't get in trouble, but of course, Jacob and I held secrets together for helping me. We knew never to make each other mad, or we would tell each other's secrets to Mom, and we both knew we didn't want Mom to find out about a lot of reckless memories of us being young and wild. It was a true strong sister and brother bond that nobody could break.

Jacob was my ride-or-die sibling. If I needed him, he was always there. We both were short-tempered. I would get in the middle of his fights, and he would protect or fight anybody who would ever cross his sissy. We still did so many things together. We went night fishing, catfishing with my dad on and off, and rode around back roads jamming to music, so I had so much hope for Jacob. I knew Jacob would be okay because he was so great and full of life every time we were together.

But as time went on, life proved me wrong. Countless nights Mom and I sat in the living room together taking care of Jacob when he was withdrawing. Seeing him shake, sweat, and moan in pain was the worst thing I had ever seen in my life. I wanted to pull that pain out of my brother's body. Mom and I had endless nights of no sleep, but we had to help Jacob. Mom and I walked up and down the driveway multiple times in the latest hours of the night to see who the hell was dropping off my brother. I watched what it did to my mom. She was slowly losing herself in the process of everything. She was going crazy and was so fed up with it. It was slowly tearing my mom apart, and she wouldn't sleep. She was always anxious and always alert about any noise she heard.

If you have never watched or helped support someone when they are withdrawing, be beyond thankful. Jacob went through rehabs and jail, but I couldn't give up faith in my brother. Rehabs were shitty and did nothing to help my brother get better. Rehabs only cared about money. Jacob would go to withdraw and sit for six days. What does six days do for someone? Nothing. Also, why do places think it's a smart thing to have a bunch of addicts together in a room with nothing for them to do? What do you think they're going to talk about? Jacob told Mom and me that you could get so many more numbers and connections to drugs and dealers. He said it was easier than we ever could imagine. It was horrible to see how many people were inside of rehabs, how many people suffered from a terrible disease, a disease that is not supported.

My mom and I went to visit Jacob in jail, and when I saw my brother like that, I just instantly broke down and started crying. I never wanted to see my brother behind a raised table wearing a one-piece suit. When he sat down, I just looked at the ground. My mom continued to talk to him and ask him questions about his time, how he had been reflecting on his life, and most importantly, how he was feeling. Jacob stopped talking and said, "Sis, look at me. I love you." I love my brother with all my heart. I felt hurt for him because he was hurting, and I didn't want my brother to hurt anymore. He told Mom and me that he needed to get out of there. That he didn't want this life for himself anymore. He swore he would change his life around and improve who he was as a person. We all three sat there hurting. His nails were bit down to his skin. We joked about Jacob telling us how crazy people were in that jail and how awful the food was. He was grateful to at least have a television in his cell because he said you literally just lay around inside the cell the entire day. When the timer rang, it meant time together was over, and we were able to hug him goodbye. Tears flowed rapidly down all three of our faces. As Jacob turned to walk away, he quickly turned around back to us and said, "I love you, Mom. Please get me out of here." It hurt so badly.

Days later, my dad took the time and went to see him also, and I imagine it made my brother beyond happy to see him. We told him that he could do this, that he needed to grow from this life lesson experience. Days later, I decided to get up and go get a tattoo about Jacob, a tattoo to remind him how much I truly love him, that no matter what, I still looked up to and honored him so much as my big brother. As I left the tattoo shop and headed home, I pulled into the driveway and saw my mom hauling ass out of the driveway. I sat in my car and called her to ensure everything was okay, and she answered, so happy and full of emotion, saying she was going to go pick up Jacob. He was out. Mom came home with him, and I showed him my tattoo; he was beyond happy. He took pictures of it and told me numerous times how much it meant to him and that he loved me so much. I felt so much joy inside my heart that I made Jacob feel worthy and reminded him that it was okay, that everyone makes mistakes, that nobody is perfect. He could pull through, overcome this blockage, and take each and every day from then on with positive actions. This setback in life could only make him stronger as a person.

Jacob became happier. He was working, saved his money, and bought his own kayak. He was so proud of himself for buying something on his own, as he should've been beyond proud. Fishing was his passion, and he started going fishing on the kayaks with my dad more often. We would play cornhole as a family; everything finally felt amazing. I got into a new relationship thanks to one of my friends for introducing me. Jacob already knew the person I started dating because they had grown up together playing baseball. They got along so well, which made me so happy. Jacob started dating my best friend at the time, so life was great. We four would hang out together, party, take rides, and go night bowling on the weekends. It was seriously such a great feeling knowing life was uplifting. To see my brother so happy meant so much to me, and I was able to have such great memories and times with him that I can hold close, knowing I had great and healthy times with Jacob. He would spend the night at my boyfriend's house with my best friend, and we would all wake up, hang out, and then party together that night.—drunk and carefree nights, healthy and pure happiness. It was awesome just to laugh and live our best lives, being young and happy. I thought to myself numerous times, *My brother is healthy. The Jacob I always knew is back.*

Summer came along. We went shark fishing. We would throw the football on the beach. The four of us would go swimming in Mom's pool. We met up at the fair with our other two stepsisters and their spouses, and at night, we would just walk around, bullshit around, being wild and young, playing carnival games, riding the rides, and just living in the moment. My mom was getting some relief. She seemed more at ease, and things were turning around for Jacob and our family. We were beyond happy and were feeling great about life and Jacob being healthy again. How could we ever fall backward again? There was no way, and we thought this was the turnaround for Jacob's health and life as we advanced in life. As his sister and someone who was always around him, I knew Jacob's body didn't have those demons inside anymore. Jacob told me, "Sis, I'm back. Thank you for allowing me to hang out with you and helping me get healthy again." That is what made me smile at the end of the day.

5

FAITH

Life continued. I moved out of my mom's house, and the signs started popping up all over again like a terrible nightmare. Jacob started bouncing from job to job, and he and his girlfriend lay in bed all day and had zero motivation to do anything. They never had any money, and they were always on the run at the most unusual times. I thought about what was happening. Then, when Jacob overdosed in my mom's driveway, reality smacked us in the face all over again. He lost his drive, his ambition of being positive and happy toward life. My best friend started changing as well. I could tell in my mom's eyes that things were getting worse. What could we do from there?

My brother and my friend split up, which was the best for both of them. My brother entered rehab. He went into rehab more and more as time passed. Many people fail to understand that going to rehab but not fully healing and receiving mental counseling for their well-being does nothing for their health long term. My brother did his damn best, he did try, and every single time our mom picked him up from rehab, he promised he would never go back.

I went with my mom to pick him up one time. He looked at my mom in the truck, and he said, "I don't want this life anymore. I'm serious." We broke out into tears, and we didn't want this for Jacob anymore. He was way too amazing as a person to go through this. What people really don't understand is that in the truck that day, Jacob would show my mom and me where drugs were in town, how to get them, where dealers left them in hidden areas, watching you pick it up and making sure you left money, and pointing out certain houses. He explained to us that certain roads were hard for him to be on. It was so sad, but it was huge reality check to Mom and me. We regained hope and faith that Jacob was going to shake this.

Unfortunately, Jacob had something inside of him, a demon that no one could understand. We didn't know how Jacob felt inside. Regardless of how much we told him how loved he was, how amazing he was, did Jacob feel like that within himself? My parents went camping all the time. Jacob went with them, and he loved it so much because he would be able to fish all weekend long. That was the time when Jacob, little brother, Mom, and our stepdad would be able to spend quality time together. But at the end of the day, my mom could tell; she could feel it. She knew Jacob wasn't still healthy and okay inside of himself. Jacob stayed in his own mind, and he never expressed to anyone how he really felt. Jacob and our younger brother would ride on the bike trails while they were camping, and Jacob would express to our little brother how he was feeling and to tell our brother he was so sorry for being on drugs and that he wasn't a big brother or a role model to him. He would tell our little brother that he would get better and that he didn't want to be an addict, but in reality, who wants to be an addict? No one, but our little brother was hurting, upset, and angry all at the same time. He loved Jacob so much, but our little brother was trying to force that brother bond between them that he had never received from Jacob.

Honestly, Jacob was trying. He tried so many times. But, again, Jacob didn't even know how to take care of his own happiness and health anymore. He loved our little brother so much but didn't really know how to express that because he was struggling so badly inside of his own thoughts. He didn't want our little brother to see him as a bad person. So it got to a point when our little brother didn't know what to say to Jacob anymore. Our little brother was also very young. He couldn't have the bond like Jacob and I had with each other. So it was difficult for him to understand what was happening. He didn't know anything about addiction, but in his eyes, he saw Jacob as his big brother, and that's what he wanted and felt like he deserved. He was absolutely right, but Jacob couldn't help that he was trying too much with being sick.

Our little brother had trusted Jacob's words, and every time, actions didn't prove anything to us that we didn't already know. It got so bad to the point that my little brother ran away from home late one night; we were devastated. When I woke up and answered my mom's phone call saying they didn't know where he was, I quickly got into my car and headed to her house. Police were already there. My mom was beyond upset. Thankfully, my little brother was found a few hours later not far away. But it was a sign, a sign that he couldn't handle much more about what was going on with Jacob and was trying to get my family's attention.

Time went on, and months grew even longer; the entire family felt defeated. We didn't know how to help Jacob any more than what we were already doing for him. Jacob always needed someone in the picture to be beside him at the end of each day. He didn't like being alone, so he continuously bounced in and out of multiple relationships. The problem that I found was that all these girls dating my brother didn't understand. They didn't grasp onto the concept that, on top of them having a lack of maturity, you could not date an addict and constantly bring them down in life for their struggle. I do believe they cared about my brother to an extent. Calling my brother an "addict" or a "piece of shit" would not help him get better; that usually calls someone to do the drug even more because they don't care about themselves anymore, and that's what happened to Jacob. These girls, knowing Jacob struggled with addiction for years, should have uplifted him. They should've tried to better him by supporting and guiding him on every day positively. It's common sense not to give an addict your debit card or car keys or even leave him alone in the car while you go inside, even if it's for five minutes. Addicts can get a drug on the street faster than you going into a store and checking out. But with a lack of knowledge and maturity, Jacob's girlfriends gave things to him because they thought that giving him what he asked and wanted was being a good girlfriend and keeping Jacob happy, which is true. Still, it wasn't helping his health or caring about his life. Sadly, they were setting my brother up for failure instead of being the stronger rock for Jacob, which he really needed. If Jacob couldn't love himself, he couldn't focus on and love another person. Girls couldn't understand that, I guess.

One girl had the nerve to post pictures of drugs she found of my brother's and bullshit pictures to tell people "her story." Excuse me, what story? You knew going into the relationship that my brother struggled with an addiction problem, and that's what you do. It was a huge joke. Luckily, I'm too grown up as an adult, so I brushed the bullshit and pettiness of these girls off. Jacob gave up his ambition, and he couldn't understand why all these girlfriends couldn't love him, why they kept leaving him and hurting him so much. It hurt my heart so badly to see my brother crying in his room, so broken each time a girl left him. He needed that person next to him in bed every night. It was Jacob's safe cushion, and every single girl left. Jacob was falling apart, and after multiple overdoses, rehabs, and even being on the street, he was too sick and unstable to realize this poison was taking over his brain, life, and body.

One day, I got off work and headed to my mom's house to drop off something for them. When I walked inside, my stepdad was downstairs, and we started chatting about life. Do you know how it feels to see your stepdad crying to you, expressing that he cannot take much trauma anymore and how hurt he is? He told me that he and my mom weren't doing well, and my stepdad asked me for advice on what to do. It hurt me so much. I hurt so much for my parents because they were such strong, incredible parents to us. I couldn't imagine being in their shoes because no one ever expects to go through this with their child.

But just when we thought we were at rock bottom with Jacob, he suddenly found a new person. This woman was older, and it seemed at the time like she had a good head on her shoulders. I thought some things were red flags about her, but everyone told me to give her a chance. She was going through a lot with her divorce, so I said, "Fine, time will tell." Jacob seemed so happy and smitten over this girl. I was happy to see my brother uplifted again, so I thought to myself, *Is this Jacob's chance to turn his life around?* She owned a restaurant. Jacob worked there 24-7 from sunrise to the latest hours of the night. I was so proud of him, and it was so good for Jacob because being busy working kept his mind occupied, and he became clean. Jacob was back to being healthy and on his own two feet.

We went to visit and spend time with him as a family. Jacob looked amazing, and he seriously glowed from a distance. His face was full, there were no marks on him, and he had gained so much weight. You could instantly tell my brother wasn't using anymore, and that felt like a huge weight off my chest. My heart was so full. You could tell by his body language he was proud of himself for taking this huge leap to change his life around.

After eating, we would walk over to Jacob and his girlfriend's house, and he was proud to show us his own place, something at the end of the day he could call his own. He saved money from working at the restaurant and bought himself a snake, the cage, lights, and any accessory he needed for the snake. He lit up with joy. He was so happy to show us the snake and everything they were redoing around the house. Jacob did this completely by himself, so for him to take the money and use it for something other than drugs, the feeling of happiness, faith, and joy was unexplainable. He showed us the rest of the house. I saw such pride and full of life in his eyes again, and that's all I ever wanted for my brother.

When Jacob would close the restaurant at night, he would call me all the time just to check up on his sissy. Through the phone, I knew Jacob was healthy. I heard it through his voice and how uplifting he was when he was on the phone. I knew he was living a positive and healthy life, and he always told me how much it meant to him for me to answer his call even though it was late. He always wanted to check in to see how my spouse and I were, how the process of our new house was going, and overall just making sure his sissy was happy. Jacob made sure his sissy was always taken care of and happy with life. I cherished every single phone call. Before every hang up, I made sure that I preached to him the same three things: that I was so beyond proud of him, to keep going day by day living a healthy lifestyle, and that I loved him so much and never to forget it.

On Christmas Eve 2020, all the siblings and spouses came to my mom and stepdad's home. My brother arrived, and he looked so handsome. Again, he looked so full of life he was glowing. He was in the best health, and Jacob was so proud to show us that he fought through addiction. He had overcome it and succeeded. Our family that night felt so alive; there was such joy and happiness. We felt it through the vibe and the atmosphere of my mom's house. We had our amazing Jacob back; I had my brother back. I felt the love through my entire body, and Jacob could really feel and could tell how proud we truly were for him.

Jacob gave our entire family gift cards that he bought on his own. The happiness that poured out of him when he was handing the gifts to us was beyond joyful and ecstatic. Of course, we didn't need any gifts from Jacob; all we wanted for him was to be healthy and be able to find himself again. That was the greatest gift we've ever received, and he proved to us that he could do it. That evening, we took family pictures, and Jacob being so happy and healthy made the pictures so beautiful and extra meaningful. It was that kind of forever moment you rarely have in life you will never forget that just simply leaves you speechless because your heart is so full of love and happiness.

But days later, the nightmare returned. I couldn't process in my head how and what was even happening. My dad, stepmom, and two sisters went to visit Jacob one afternoon for lunch at his restaurant so that he could finally meet his new baby sister. As we pulled up and walked inside, I noticed Jacob wasn't there. So I simply asked out loud, "Where's my brother?"

This random guy answered back, saying, "Oh, are you Jake's family?"

I felt that something was odd, so I said, "Yes, why?"

In return, I received a snippy comment back: "I don't want any problems. Jake isn't here. He's over at the house."

Confused and feeling like there was something off in this situation, I walked over to the house, went inside, and saw my brother sitting in a chair at the table. A huge knot filled my stomach when I looked at his face because I saw a depressed and broken person. Listening to the situation that had occurred that day between him and his girlfriend, I knew Jacob was not in the wrong. His girlfriend was a horrible person for doing this to my brother, for doing disgusting things behind his back with other men. I was standing there thinking, *Is this woman really doing this nasty shit while dating my brother?* I was livid. Jacob had been drinking all day, depressed and alone. He had been dealing with the issue for a while. Sadly, because he loved this woman he just dealt with what she was doing. My protective side when it came to Jacob instantly kicked in, and I started going off. But his girlfriend was pretty damn slick. She was smooth, and the words coming out of her mouth flowed out like butter. She said my brother had been doing drugs again, that everything Jacob said she was doing with other men was a lie. The conversation escalated. Yelling and nonstop arguing, she walked out of the house. Jacob was so defeated. He tried to explain everything to us, and what hurt even worse was that Jacob was not lying about anything he had said to us. Struggling and having a hard time with the day, Jacob asked our dad three times to please get him out of that house and let him leave with us. The answer from my dad was, "No, son. I have to go to work soon." It was a forever image, a giant demon I will forever face in my mind for the rest of my life. I saw through Jacob's eyes how hurt he was when we walked out of the house to leave and close the door on him. We left, and my brother had to stay in that hellhole. I should've stayed with him, and I didn't. I let myself down, and I let my brother down. That was selfish of me, but at that exact moment in time, I didn't know what that night was going to bring. Now I feel like a piece of shit because of it, and I will forever blame myself.

I called my mom, the parent who would never, never once say no to her children. She and my step-dad drove to Jacob. They begged him for over forty-five minutes to please get in their truck and go home with them, but he wouldn't. He only wanted to go with my dad. Later that night, my brother was arrested for something that wasn't his fault and could've been completely avoided if my dad would've just let Jacob go with him. But my dad didn't care about Jacob the way he honestly should have.

Jacob fell apart; he was shattered, hurt, and mentally broken. From that day on, my brother lost himself and gave up on life. Our mom got Jacob out of jail and brought him home to her house. He was shattered, and we all knew it. From there, we learned to spend as much time as we possibly could with Jacob. Heartbroken, we knew Jacob wasn't going to be with us forever. His demons grew more extensive, and it hurt beyond hell to see someone we loved so much fall apart, knowing we couldn't save him or help make him feel different about himself or about life. Jacob went back to using severely, and nothing we said mattered; he told us numerous times he didn't love himself, and he wished we would just leave him alone. We couldn't do that, and we fought to fix and help Jacob as much as we possibly could; my mom did *everything* for him.

My mom begged Jacob to please stop. He was crushing my mom's heart. My mom called me every single day, and we would talk about Jacob and what we should do. I would ask her every day how Jacob was doing. She would text me at all times of the day, especially at night, because she could never sleep. She lived and stayed worried 24-7, and her anxiety never stopped. But then, a dear friend of our family reached out to Jacob and wanted to give him an opportunity to work for his fencing company. He wanted to provide

Jacob with a chance at life, and to take him under his wing meant so much to my family, especially my mom. Jacob didn't have any other friends because everyone had given up on my brother because they looked at him with disgust.

But Jacob flourished; he woke up every day from that moment on and worked all day with him. Jacob was so happy. He loved talking about the jobs they were working on and was excited to wake up to something new on the job every day. Of course, in the back of my mom's mind, she was worried because Jacob working meant money in his wallet. But she knew she couldn't tell him no. He was getting up every day and happy to work with a good friend, but my mom knew what the money would go toward instead of savings. To my mom, that felt like someone stabbing her in the heart, knowing my brother was taking hard-earned cash and hurting his body in return. Jacob, for some reason, at the end of every day, wanted to feel numb so that he didn't have to hear or feel the demons inside of him taking over his brain and body. It was the quickest solution. But that is what hurt us the damn most. We didn't understand why Jacob didn't feel like he was worthy enough, the way we saw him—so beyond amazing as a man. My mom called rehab after rehab. She tried multiple states, she tried everything. The rehabs had the nerve to tell my mom that Jacob was not considered "high risk." They told my mom Jacob was not able to come into their rehabs because he wasn't severe enough. The next day, my brother overdosed. My mom texted the rehab agent that she had been texting back and forth with for week to try and convince him to let Jacob go into the facility. The guy responded to my mom saying, "I'm sorry to hear that." What a damn joke. Rehabs aren't there to help; it's for money. My brother was denied help numerous times. So how was my brother supposed to ever become clean and healthy if rehabs treated people like this? Jacob told Mom and me that the people who work in rehabs treat you like shit anyways.

6

BROKEN HEART

On Friday, February 26, 2021, at around eight at night, my spouse and I were sitting by the bonfire at our house having a much-needed weekend drink as my phone lit up with a text message from my mom. Jacob wasn't well, and his health was getting a lot worse. She said Jacob just didn't care about himself anymore, he didn't have any emotion toward life, and he didn't care what we thought about it. She said I just deserved to know. I sat there staring at my phone and decided to go inside for the night. I came inside and typed a four-page text message to my brother, pouring my heart out to him about every devastating emotion I felt toward him, drugs, and the entire situation. I needed to let him know how I felt, how much he meant to me, that he needed to be strong, that he could overcome this— the list went on. Tears rolled down my face and I tried to finish typing to him, and I needed him to know how much he meant to me. He responded, "Thank you for reaching out to me, sis. I will talk to you soon, okay? I love you so much—your big brother, Jake." Little did I know that would be the last text message I would ever receive from my brother.

February 28 was Jacob's twenty-seventh birthday. The entire day, nobody in the family heard from Jacob. I texted my mom numerous times throughout the entire day, asking her, "Have you heard from Jacob?"

I always got the same response: "No, have you?" The constant messages back and forth to my mom continued into the late hours of the night. I asked my spouse so many times, "Babe, do you think Jacob's okay?"

He kept responding, "He's fine, honey. He probably just wants to be alone on his birthday today, or maybe he doesn't have any minutes on his phone. Don't worry so much."

My head rushed a thousand thoughts every minute that ticked by that day. My dad texted me, asking for Jacob to call him back because he had been trying to reach him all day so he could pick my brother up to go fishing. I couldn't tell him that no one had heard from him. I didn't know what to say back to my dad besides "Okay, Pops. I will let him know."

That night, I sat in bed staring at the ceiling. I had so much anxiety, and I turned my phone off vibrate and on to sound, hoping I would hear it ding at any moment. I just needed to see it light up showing a text from "Big Brother," but it never did.

I woke up the next morning after sleeping for maybe a total of an hour, and I felt like there was a hole in my heart. I told my spouse I didn't feel very well at all. Something was just not right, and I felt it through my entire body. He replied, saying that maybe I should just stay home today. But I didn't. I dragged myself out of bed and went to work.

I quickly texted my Mom, asking her if she had heard from Jacob yet. The answer was, "No, I didn't." I sat at my work desk, telling my coworkers how the weekend went, how much I hoped and prayed that Jacob was okay, and that hopefully, my mom or myself would hear from Jacob sometime that morning or at least some point that day. I continued with work with an empty pit in my stomach. At 11:30 a.m., my phone went off. I had kept my phone on sound that entire morning so I could quickly get to it. I grabbed my phone, and it was a message from my little brother saying, "You work today, don't you?"

I responded, "Yes, why? What's up?" I just figured my little brother needed to come to my house for something because he was always at my house and a lot of his things always stayed there. He texted me back, saying, "You need to come to Mom's house after work."

"Why?" I replied back as quickly as I could. With no response, I texted again, "What's wrong?"

Finally, his response back was, "You might want to call Mom. I don't want to tell you over a text or over the phone."

I knew right then. I knew in my heart what that meant. I felt it through my entire body in seconds. Shaking, I looked at my coworker. I said, "I need to call my brother. Something's wrong."

So I had another coworker walk down to the classroom so I could step out. I walked into the hallway and called my little brother. I called him three times—no answer at all. I called my mom. When my mom answered the phone, I heard it through her broken voice.

She said, "Selena, give somebody your phone. I need to talk to them."

Yelling, I called my coworker to the hallway. She grabbed my phone and started walking in the opposite direction. As she turned back around, I saw her face and her eyes full of pain. She told me, "I need you to get your bags, and I'm going to drive you to your mom's house."

With tears quickly building up heavily in my eyes, I put hand over my heart and said, "Tell me right now. Did my brother pass away? I need to know right now."

My coworker, fighting to hold back her tears, her eyes full of hurt, and hesitating to say anything, just nodded her head. I dropped to my knees in the hallway. In that second, everything around me turned black and silent, and I felt nothing. I was numb and empty, crying and shaking. I quickly went into the classroom and grabbed my bags. My other coworkers gave me a quick hug as tears rolled down my cheeks. I couldn't even come to terms with what was actually happening. I told my coworker I wanted to drive myself to my mom's because I needed to call my spouse. But when he answered, troubled by not knowing what to even say to me, I learned my mom had already called him and told him the horrible news. My coworker followed behind me to ensure that I got to my mom's house safely.

I walked into my mom's house and walked straight back to my little brother's bedroom. He was under his blanket crying hysterically and couldn't look at me. Feeling so shattered, I walked out and sat on the chair and just stared at the floor with my hands folded together, tapping my foot over and over again, watching tears fall on my pants. I felt my heart beating through my chest one hundred miles per second as I watched my mom and stepdad pulling into the driveway. As my mom walked into the house, reality set into my brain that this was happening. My brother was gone. She bent over and gave a tight, silent hug. The tears were endless. My stepsister and her wife pulled into the house and walked in shortly after.

As a family, we all sat in the living room feeling empty in this black hole of hurt. I was sitting on the floor, foot tapping, hands shaking terribly, and countless thoughts rushing through every bone in my body. My dad called my mom, and he could barely catch his breath. His voice hurt me to hear, saying over and over again the same words, "Crystal...not our son, this isn't true. My baby boy, not my baby boy." It was awful. My spouse quickly got to the house, and he could see we were completely shattered. He couldn't even say anything because, really, what could he say to our family? It's something we'd had nightmares about, had prayed for years to please watch over Jacob and to please give him time and let him fight this battle. It was something we had always dreaded and news we never wanted to receive. At that moment, we weren't strong enough to process it. Seeing my little brother stand at the back door, just looking outside with tears rolling down his face, hurt me so much. I had never seen him show emotion, and it hurt my heart. I stood next to him with my arm around him, but I couldn't say anything because I couldn't come up with the right words. When we were staring at my mom's backyard, I realized that our lives and our family would never be the same ever again. It truly felt like hell.

My little sister called me, and she told me it couldn't be true. She was hurting so much, and I couldn't handle hearing her cry through the phone. My mom was sitting on the couch in the living room, and her phone kept going off. It seemed like the ringer was stuck on repeat for as long as it kept going off. It was starting to make me mad because I thought it wasn't polite for people to reach out to my family so quickly; we didn't even have time to tell our own family members or close friends before the media took over. It really pissed me off. I shut my phone off, and I just couldn't deal with it. I stayed at my mom's house for a few hours. They were silent hours. It hurt me so much to stand up to give my mom a hug and kiss goodbye. I felt guilty leaving. I couldn't believe my mom had just lost her son, and I hurt for her so much because I didn't understand how she felt inside. My mom literally lost her baby, the person who had made her a mother. My heart hurt so badly for my mom.

I got into my car and drove home, and I played Jacob's song, the one we shared together, on repeat until I saw my driveway. Sitting in my car, I just sat, numb, staring at my house, and I prayed. I prayed for my mom, hoping that she would be strong enough to fight through this horrible pain with so much faith.

I'm not a parent yet, but I will tell you I felt her pain when I gave my mom that hug goodbye. I knew this would affect her more than anyone else because my mom had tried for years to help Jacob pull through this. My mom was the one who saved Jacob for years. My mom never gave up on him. My mom loved Jacob so much, and she would tell me every day that she was scared Jacob wasn't going to be here much longer with us. Now we were living this nightmare, and I was so worried for my mom. I let my dog outside, and he knew immediately that something was wrong with his mommy. He tried giving me a hug, putting his paws up on my shoulders, and would not leave my side. He hates when I cry, so he tried to kiss every bit of the tears rolling off my face to take care of his mommy. My spouse and I then left to go check on my dad, sister and stepmom. As we pulled in the driveway and walked into his house, you could have heard a pin drop. My dad was on the couch, head down and hands folded. He completely lost it and kept saying, "Why my baby boy?" My sister came upstairs and sat on the floor, holding onto Jacob's picture and rereading messages between her and Jacob she had on her phone. It was the worst feeling I had ever felt.

Later that night, we headed home; I didn't do anything. I thought I was going to get sick any second. Dragging my feet, I got into the shower with the hot water pouring down on me. I stood there with my hands against the shower wall and just let out any emotion I had left inside of me. I cried until I couldn't cry anymore, talking to God in the shower, asking him *why my brother?* I wasn't coming to an understanding. I thought there was no way this could be happening to my family. But furthermore, why is this happening to my mom? She was the most incredible mom ever, and I couldn't understand how this could happen. As I got out of the shower, my spouse and I took our dog out for the last time before bed. I was looking up at the sky, and there was this one star, a star that sparkled a little differently from the rest. It shone beyond bright. I stared at it; something in my heart told me that it was Jacob. I pointed up and showed my spouse. We both stood there for about five minutes, silently holding onto each other as our tears connected together, falling down from our faces. For the rest of the night, I lay next to my spouse on the couch as he held me extra tight to ensure I knew he was there for me. My body was endlessly shaking, my phone constantly buzzing. I couldn't even look at the television screen, and everything seemed like a blur. I couldn't have asked for a better spouse that night. Going to sleep that night, I just stared at the ceiling. Our room was dark and black, and that's how I felt inside. Empty with a hole in my heart. I stayed awake texting my mom, wondering how are we were going to get through this.

7

FACING REALITY

I felt so lost. I felt like I had nothing inside of me; every emotion and every feeling I thought I could feel was gone. I dreaded making myself get up out of bed the following day. My dog wouldn't leave my sight. He felt and knew something was wrong with his mommy. I immediately walked outside once I got out of bed and looked up at the sky. I just stood and talked to Jacob, pouring out to him every single emotion I felt inside of me. It wasn't fair. Why my brother? I came inside and texted my mom. I got dressed and headed to her house.

The drive there, I thought to myself, *Here is the sun shining into my car. The worst moment in our lives happened yesterday, and yet we have to get up and face life because life doesn't just get to pause.* I got to my mom's and walked inside, and everyone looked empty. We were lost; we didn't have any words for each other, so we sat silently. The next few days continued the exact same way, and everything seemed like a complete blur. The number of people who reached out to our family was endless. The sympathies, gifts, dinners, and flowers were huge. The number of things my family received towered and took over my mom's house. It was overwhelming at times, but I knew it was only good from people's hearts. One of Jacob's childhood best friends drove from DC just to come and give his sympathy to our family. He sat at the dining table looking through pictures with my mom and me and reminisced on so many memories he was able to have with Jacob. It brought joy to the room, and I was so happy my brother could have so many great times with a great friend. He showed us on his phone how many times he and Jacob reached out to each other just to chat about life and to catch up with one another. It was so lovely to see that a true friend actually checked up on my brother often. He had never given up on my brother, and he didn't even live close to us, so that spoke volumes about him as a friend to my brother. He was always there to just listen to Jacob and to give him advice and support, and it meant so much to my mom and me to see.

Time ticked by silently. My family from North Carolina came up immediately, and they helped my mom so much. Setting everything up and anything else they could possibly take out of my mom's hands they did, and I know it took so much weight off of my mom's shoulders. I couldn't be any more grateful for all the support my family received, but it was beyond hard to be present at the time. My entire body felt numb. I felt like my body was just standing with no emotion, and I was sick and tired of hearing "Your brother wouldn't want to see you like this." Nobody had the damn right to tell me how I should be feeling. At the time, I felt the best way to go through each day was to do the bare minimum, just to hold everything I was feeling inside of me. Nobody understood how it felt for me. I walked into my mom's house and saw my brother's things sitting on the dining table. His glove, baseballs, and stuff I had bought him as gifts for encouragement and trying my absolute best to ensure that I was always there for him just stared me down physically and mentally. One gift was a plaque that said, *You got this, one day at a time; I love you, brother— your sis, Selena.* Another plaque I got him said, *You are capable of amazing things.* Jacob told me once that he had hung it right next to his closet to remind himself every day when he got dressed. To see that sitting there out in open felt like a knife going through my heart. I sat there for hours looking through old pictures, hundreds of photos of Jacob and I growing up, memories I had with him that I had forgotten about. To see them all over again made me hurt even worse. I stayed at my mom's all day and went home around the time people would start getting off of work and showing up at my mom's. I just couldn't handle seeing any more people other than my own family members crying and trying to comfort me. I am a stubborn person. I wouldn't say I like hugging and being all lovey in moments when I feel like hell.

Two days went by, and I lay in bed from countless days of no sleep and decided to go through Jacob's entire Facebook page. Seeing stupid shit that dealers had written about my brother made me sick and beyond pissed. It fueled a fire inside of me. Over six different times, my brother had him and me as his profile picture. One caption even said, "Love taking pictures with my baby sis." Chills ran down my spine, knowing Jacob would never be able to say that again. Knowing Jacob and I will never be able to take another picture together. Also realizing I'll never be able to grow older with my big brother. I kept scrolling down on his page.

I had never realized how often Jacob talked about me. Saying how much he would always be there for me. Asking others for prayers when I had my terrible car accident, writing how much he truly loved me, especially when my birthday came every year. It hurt seeing comments Jacob had written on my pictures; I'll never see that again. But what pissed me off the most was how many people were on my brother's page and had seen that my brother put numerous quotes up talking about how lost and depressed he was, and no one reached out to my brother. Besides family, you didn't see anyone comment to give my brother any form of advice or just to say "I'm here if you need to talk." Nothing. It's bullshit. All these people could post something when he passed away, but why didn't they worry about my brother when he was struggling so badly?

Later that day, my dad and stepmom came over to my mom's house, and my mom, stepdad, dad, stepmom, and myself all sat together at the dining table to discuss what the plans were going forward for Jacob. It was so lovely being able to see my mom and dad come together. They put their differences with each other to the side because, at the time, nothing else mattered besides Jacob. My dad and my mom hugged each other and cried, and it broke my heart. Jacob made them parents, and now they were sitting having to talk about what to do with their son who was no longer here. You should never have to bury and say goodbye to your child.

The following day, we had to go set up Jacob's services at the funeral home as a family. As we got inside and sat down, my heart started racing and feeling beyond heavy as the man in charge of the funeral home started talking to us about what our plans for Jacob were. I became very irritated and uncomfortable. I didn't want to sit down and talk about what we were doing with my brother's body, and I didn't even want to believe Jacob was gone. I didn't want to hold anyone's hands, nothing. I just stared straight ahead. In fact, the man told me I was "a very quiet person." We continued to discuss what was going to be written for Jacob's obituary for the newspaper. We had to pick out a poem that we felt was right for Jacob to have in his pamphlet for people to have when walking into the funeral and to decide the main picture for his cover. It was so painful to talk about, but we decided that Jacob was going to be cremated. Talking about my brother felt disgusting—only twenty-seven years old and already taken from this thing we call life.

As we walked outside after being finished, I realized I wasn't okay with a decision we had made inside. My parents asked me what was wrong. I felt like it wasn't fair for people who just left, gave up, and walked away from my brother to have the right to see my brother for the last time. I yelled, "No, they don't get to see my brother. They don't deserve to." All of Jacob's so-called "friends" gave up on him once he started struggling with addiction, and I have nothing nice to say to them at all. It would've taken ten minutes to go to my mom's house, sit my brother down on the steps, and ask him how he was doing, how he felt, if he needed anything, or simply to just support Jacob in general, but nope. Besides our family, everyone turned their back on my brother—everyone. Once I had my meltdown outside, yelling and quickly turning upset, my family understood where I was coming from and agreed with me. My stepdad started crying as he listened to me getting so upset; he then walked inside to ask the man to change Jacob's services to private. It meant so much to me for my stepdad to go inside and for my family to accept how I felt. We decided in the parking lot that the funeral would be for family only and close friends to our family.

The night before his funeral, we decided we would just set something up for the public to come and to give their condolences and respect to my family, as well as to celebrate Jacob's life for how amazing he, indeed, was. When we got back to my mom's house, my mom gave me the honor to pick out Jacob's outfit, the very last outfit we will ever see him in. It was the easiest decision. I went to my brother's closet and picked out what represented my brother the best. I wanted Jacob to look exactly like himself—blue jeans, a T-shirt, a hoodie, and a Ravens hat. It felt horrible to touch my brother's clothes. They smelled just like him, and I couldn't get his smell out of my nose for the rest of the night. Nothing and no one will ever replace his scent.

As the week went forward, it was hard to split time between my mom and dad. It was hard enough to balance my own emotions, but I helped my mom put together picture boards of our family with Jacob and created a picture board with his friends. Then, I went to my dad's house to help my little sister make a Williams family board with Jacob. We needed the boards for the night of my brother's celebration event. It was such a struggle to look at so many pictures of seeing my brother so damn happy and doing things he enjoyed doing, seeing his bright and beautiful smile in the images of when he caught his giant catfish when he was living his best life.

The next day, March 5th, was absolutely terrible, starting from morning to the very end. My mom wrote a heartbreaking message to my brother. I went to my mom's house, and she gave me Jacob's lighter to have forever. He only used one skull lighter always. Then, once my spouse came home from work, we went to my dad's house to attempt to eat dinner, but it turned into a wreck. My dad was loading up the dishwasher, and he had a mental breakdown. He started yelling out loud, grabbed his truck keys, and hauled ass going out of the driveway. My stepmom was so upset. My dad didn't take his cell phone, so we had no way to contact him or know where the hell he was going. My spouse and I sat around to support my stepmom, but almost an hour had already gone by, and it was getting late. We needed to head home. Once we got home, I received a text message from my mom saying that my dad was there at her house. My dad got out of his truck and asked my stepdad to come outside to talk to him. My dad went there to apologize to my mom and stepdad for not being a good dad or being there for Jacob and me, thanking my stepdad for taking care of Jacob and me when my dad should've done more for Jacob, and now it was too late. He and my stepdad sat outside on the tailgate and let out raw emotions they had built up inside of them. My dad told my stepdad that he regretted so many things and that Jacob would've lost his life years ago if it wasn't for my stepdad and my mom. My mom and stepdad saved Jacob and took care of him with everything they had and had done everything possible to keep Jacob safe and alive.

About thirty minutes later, my mom texted me, saying my dad was pulling out of her driveway, so I texted my stepmom to let her know that dad was okay and that he should be heading her way. My spouse and I were outside letting our dog out, and I was going to talk to Jacob's star to tell him good night when we suddenly heard a vehicle in front of our house. It was just standing still in the road, but when we walked up front to see who it was, the vehicle sped off, squealing tires. But then we heard the vehicle making a U-turn in the road and it came back toward our house. My spouse took our dog inside and told me to wait and see who it was because we already figured it was probably my dad. My dad came pulling into my driveway. I walked up front, and he was crying so hard, saying he missed Jacob, that he was a horrible father, and that he was going to kill himself when he left my mom's house because he said he deserved to be gone and not Jacob. Instead, thankfully he drove to my house to talk and see me for a few minutes. Do you know how it feels to hear your own dad tell you that he is going to kill himself? It's awful, especially because I still couldn't even process my brother being gone, and now my dad thought he deserved to be gone for mistakes and regrets for past times that he couldn't undo. Over and over again, my dad told me he wanted to trade spots with Jacob and that he couldn't do this. He didn't know if he could live on with Jacob not being here anymore. I felt beyond sick to my stomach. Luckily, about forty minutes later, I was able and strong enough to support, help, and guide my dad to make the right decision just to go home and go to sleep. I asked him if he wanted me to get into my car and follow him until he got to his house. But he said no. He promised me on everything that he would drive straight home. So, with a long hug, my dad pulled out of the driveway and headed home. I texted my stepmom, letting her know Dad should be there in a couple of minutes, and exactly five minutes later, she texted me, letting me know that he was home. I was so over the day. I was ready for the nightmare to stop, but the nightmare only grew larger and followed us into the next day.

March 6, 2021, was the day of Jacob's celebration. We had a place rented out for a couple of hours for people to come in and out, the time only to show up to give their condolences and respect for my brother's life. My spouse and I were drained, and I was defeated. It had been days of complete hell, so we stayed home all morning to collect our mental health and to rest for a while. Early that afternoon, we had to start getting ready because I needed to go to my mom's house first to go through a book of how I wanted Jacob's ashes for myself when I heard my cell phone going off. So I ran out to the kitchen and saw it was my mom calling me. I answered the phone, and it was my uncle saying, "Don't freak out. Everything's okay." My little brother had been driving his truck heading home when his entire truck caught on fire. He barely made it to the driveway of my mom's house, flew out of his driver's side door, the truck struck a tree in my mom's yard, and the entire truck blew up. My little brother had literally been on fire and had been rushed to the hospital. I was shaking uncontrollably, yelling to my spouse that we needed to leave immediately. My spouse drove as fast as he could while still trying to be safe. We couldn't pull into my mom's driveway. Numerous fire trucks and police vehicles were putting out my brother's truck. Once we were able to get into the driveway, I needed to get to my mom immediately. I went upstairs, and I hurt so badly for her as soon as I saw her face. She couldn't even get herself dressed. She was fed up with life, not understanding why our family was going through so much trauma in one week. She looked at me and said, "I almost lost another child in the same week." She held onto me, giving me a tight hug, rocking each other back and forth, saying to me, "Selena, what the hell is happening? Our family cannot take much more before I have a mental breakdown. I cannot do this." I helped my mom get together, and we left to go to Jacob's celebration. My mom felt so guilty for feeling like she had to choose whether to go to the hospital to be with my little brother or to the celebration. I told her she could not feel like that and that my little brother wouldn't want our mom to feel guilty. So my cousin followed the ambulance and sat with my little brother the entire time until he was released. Her doing that for my mom and us meant so much more than we could ever explain. I didn't want my little brother to think we weren't there to support him. I was beyond worried about him; I couldn't focus or sit still. When we pulled up to the celebration, my little brother called me. He told me to stop crying, he was okay, and that Jacob was giving him a sign saying he wasn't going anywhere. He said that Jacob had thrown him out of the truck so he didn't burn up because he swore he didn't remember jumping out of the truck. He said he would be there in about an hour. He was already cleared besides waiting on arm X-ray results, but he was completely fine besides a few minor burns. I was so relieved, especially for my mom and stepdad. I knew they couldn't handle much more trauma that week.

As we walked into the celebration, I didn't know what to expect, but it was gorgeous to stand still, look around, and see how amazing Jacob indeed was. At the tables were our picture boards, Jacob's sports jerseys, medals, ribbons, and trophies. He had about a hundred awards. There were his Ravens and Phillies banners and his blankets, decorations from his bedroom, boards designed for people to write on, and a massive picture of my brother with angel wings on his back. The image actually looked like he was walking up to heaven. I stood there, silent for a moment, with tears falling onto the floor. I couldn't come to reality inside of my own mind that we were here because my brother no longer was. My little brother arrived, and he smelled like he was burnt. His hair was literally fried, and he showed me his burns on his back, and he had his wrist and hand wrapped. I was so thankful to see my brother in front of me and to know he was okay. I gave him a huge hug. I just didn't realize how precious life really was until this week happened to my family. As the doors opened, a massive line of people started to walk in with music playing in the background, songs that the family made into a playlist that reminded us of Jacob. A group of guys wore Superman shirts in honor of my brother. As the family stood off to the side together, people circled around, glancing at the tables celebrating Jacob's life. It brought a lot of people joy looking at old pictures of memories they had with him. Then, in the end, people would come to hug my family with deep sympathy and a lot of heartbreaks. I felt like I was two different personalities that night. I was so honored that so many people came to show support for Jacob. It was amazing to see that my brother was loved and had many great times with so many people in many different ways. Still, I was also beyond irritated and pissed off the more I watched people come inside the celebration. I couldn't understand why they could come to this event, but they couldn't have checked on my brother throughout the years he struggled. When I watched specific individuals walk inside, I thought to myself, *Now you show up, but when my brother really needed you, you stopped being his friend because he was an addict.* The petty excuse I heard for years from Jacob's "friends" was "it was too hard to be around him, seeing him like that," or "I didn't know what to do for him anymore." Complete bullshit, and it ran through my mind throughout the rest of the event. I was ready to get it over with so that I could just get into the truck and go home with my spouse because he could tell I wasn't thrilled. The time for the event was over, and we all walked to our vehicles. I gave my family huge hugs, knowing that tomorrow was going to be far worse. I was beyond exhausted mentally, and I felt like I was just awake at this point, not even knowing how I was functioning. So my spouse and I went home for the night to rest up before tomorrow's nightmare.

8

FOREVER DEMONS

On March 7, 2021, I woke up knowing that day would be one of the most challenging days of my entire life. It was the day I was going to have to tell my big brother goodbye, the very last time I would ever be able to see his handsome face in person until one day when I see him again in heaven. I felt sick to my stomach, knowing that was what I was waking up to do that day. I couldn't even talk. I just went outside once I got out of bed and talked to Jacob. Then I came inside to eat some breakfast because I was scared that I would literally get sick if I didn't. After making my spouse and me breakfast, we got ready and headed to the funeral home. I cried the entire way going there, not understanding why this was happening to my family right now and why my brother because he was so damn incredible.

As we pulled into the parking lot of the funeral home, I saw my little brother walking down the ramp from being inside the funeral home, bawling his eyes out, and right then, reality hit me right in the face. My spouse and I walked in, and staring right in front of my face was Jacob's casket. I walked forward, and when I saw Jacob's face, I held onto his casket and dropped to my knees. I felt like the air was sucked out of my lungs. I was nothing at that moment. I looked at his beautiful face. His freckles were clear as day. Everything looked the same, like he was just taking a nap or something, and I just cried, holding onto my mom and dad. It hurt worse looking at my brother, and he literally looked just fine. That was a slap in the face. My mom had me sit down, and I felt glued to my chair for most of the time. People continued to walk in and out to see my brother. I was beyond pissed when I realized my dad had invited some of Jacob's old friends when they looked at Jacob like a piece of trash for multiple years. I thought we had all decided together as a family that no one besides family was to be at the funeral. I was pissed, but it wasn't even the time. I had gotten up a few more times to stand alone with my brother for the last time.

I touched his face, kissed his forehead, and held onto his hand even though they were icy cold. I didn't care. I literally wanted to warm them back up for him again. My mom came up to me, and we stood there together talking to Jacob, and we fixed his hair to make his hair look more like Jacob would always have it done. My brother was going to be at peace looking just like himself. My little brother came up along with us, and then following behind him was our Grandfather. It broke me to see my grandfather so upset and to see how hurt he was to see my mom so broken. It was the worst pain I had ever experienced.

Sitting back in the chair, I looked around for a minute. My spouse was crying, my siblings were destroyed, and my parents looked literally defeated. I could feel my mom's hurt all the way from across the room, but I couldn't imagine looking at your own child in that way. The crying never stopped. Darkness and hurt filled that entire room.

As the time came to an end with my brother, the room was left only for my parents and siblings. My little brother walked up, kneeling down and saying his last words to Jacob, crying so badly. My little sister got up, walked up next to my little brother, and wrapped her arm around him as they both stood up there talking to Jacob together. It was the saddest image ever to see. I walked up to be with them and held on to them both. I told both of them how much Jacob loved them and to please never forget that because he will forever watch over them both. As they said their final words, they walked away, and I was left standing with my big brother, just him and me, one last time. I held onto Jacob's hand and kissed his forehead, and I told him how much I loved him, how much I looked up to him, and how honored I was that I was his little sister. I told him thank you for being the best big brother to me and that our bond with each other would never be replaceable. I promised him that I would talk to him every day and forever tell him goodnight. I would make him proud as his sister, and I hoped he will see me get everything I've always dreamed of every day he wakes up. I told him to fly high, do whatever he wants, whatever will make him happy, and to love every single piece of himself. My feet felt stuck to the ground. As I gave him a final kiss and goodbye, my spouse came up and helped me walk away. But, walking away, I knew a piece of me was just left up at that casket with Jacob and that I would never gain that missing piece of my heart ever again.

My parents came out about ten minutes after, and they didn't speak or look at anyone. I walked over to my mom's passenger side window and just told her that

I loved her and that I would see her a little bit later for family dinner. Later that day, my spouse and I went over for dinner. It was actually nice to be around family love and for all of us to be together supporting each other's hurt and emptiness because everyone felt the exact same way with one huge demon inside of us.

The following week, I took off the entire time and spent every day with my mom. There were a few days when she and I just sat around her house talking, and there came a day when I would pull into the driveway of her house, and I would see my mom crying in her truck. Other times she would be sitting at my brother's bench in the front yard. She would be so at a loss for words and hurt so badly. It sucked because, honestly, I didn't know what to say to her sometimes. After all, I didn't know how my mom felt. It was horrible to have my mom look at me and say, "Selena, I'm so sorry." My mom had nothing to be sorry for, but she held every bit of what happened to Jacob on her shoulders. It was not her fault, but I couldn't tell her otherwise. She didn't want to hear it.

Days later, my mom and I took time from reality and spent the day together at the beach to share some much-needed smiles and laughs. Being at the house, we were stuck in a black hole. It was depressing because every day for weeks, my mom's house still received nonstop deliveries. Even though it was thoughtful, my mom's house started looking like a funeral home all over again. Flower arrangements took over the living room. But as the week slowly came to an end, my mom and I knew reality was coming, going back to work. That Monday, mom and I went back to work. My mom texted me, saying she was sitting in her truck parked at work and she didn't know if she could get out, and I assured her that it was okay. Anything she could do was enough and to never forget that. My mom was beyond strong, and she went inside work. She worked all week. Every day, we would message each other to check in saying, "Thinking of you," and instead of saying have a good day, we would say "have a day," because, really, was a "good" day even possible anymore? As the days went on, emotions grew larger and harder with Jacob actually being gone.

For a month, I was in a bad state of mind. I could get through work fine because I worked with kids, so I didn't really have time to sit and think about my own personal issues, but once I was off and at home, everything I bundled inside of me would lash out at night, especially on the weekends. I took so much out on my spouse, and I knew I shouldn't have done that, but I did because I was hurting and didn't realize anything else around me was getting affected by it. I said many hurtful things, and I guess it was because I wanted him to feel the hurt that I felt. I didn't understand why he wasn't hurting the way I was hurting. It was selfish of me. But at the time, I was only thinking of myself and my family. Looking back after the first month of Jacob being gone, my spouse was my rock, and I couldn't be any more grateful for the man I have in my life for being there every single time I was falling and going through a lot of mental instability. It speaks volumes of who he is as a person. He saw me struggle through so much, but he also saw how broken my parents were. He supported me through every struggle when I would go off about how unfair life was. Every single time, he would let me go off and then say, "Babe, it's okay, and it's also okay to let it all out." I wouldn't've gotten through a lot of black demons inside of me if I didn't have him by my side every day, and I'm so thankful for that man.

As Easter came along, I knew holidays would never feel the same. That morning, my mom started her day at Jacob's favorite fishing spot to watch the sunrise, and she texted me, asking, "Do you believe in reincarnation?" With no question asked back, I simply answered yes. Later, I went to my mom's for Easter dinner, and my mom told me that when she was at Jacob's spot that morning, a fish kept jumping out of the water while she was talking to Jacob the entire time. I told her it was a sign from Jacob. I told my mom Jacob was telling her that he loves and misses her so much and to have a good Easter.

The next day, my mom and I spent another great day together shopping. When we went out to lunch, my little brother met us there, and while we were eating, my mom said, "Give me a bite-bite." My little brother and I immediately looked at each other and smiled because that is what Jacob always said, and at that moment it really felt like Jacob was sitting at the table with us.

As weeks went on, my parents' struggles continued to grow. My mom told me how much she missed Jacob's voice. She missed his smile. She missed his smell, his hugs, his jokes, and how he used to make her feel. It was awful. I missed Jacob so much too, but not the way my mom did. She missed his everything. As a family, we all went to the beach for my mom's birthday, and we took all the flowers we had received from people for Jacob's passing. Instead of throwing them away, we walked out to one of Jacob's favorite fishing spots and threw the flowers into the ocean. My mom and I threw them as hard as we could, smiling and crying at the same time, telling Jacob how much we loved him, that we would miss him forever, and to remember just to enjoy and take care of himself. It was a beautiful moment.

Once at home again, my mom and stepdad received a beautiful gift from Jacob. The friend who Jacob had worked with installing fences dropped something off on my mom's step, a piece of wood from Jacob's last project that he had ever worked on at the job. It was amazing. The friend had it engraved for our family and told us he really felt like Jacob had so much more to offer and he would surely be missed. It meant so much to my family, and it spoke volumes about that friend. We knew he was one of the few people who actually cared for my brother and rooted for him every day. He had always looked at my brother the exact same way we did, a great man, and he gave my brother that chance at life, knowing how amazing Jacob was and how much potential he had. He also gave my mom Jacob's work shirt, and it brought us to tears. Jacob was bright, hardworking, and so smart. I thank that one friend for giving my brother a chance to get healthy and for always being a friend to talk and lean on when my brother needed him.

After two months of Jacob being gone, my family was able to pick him up. As if grieving wasn't hard enough, to actually hold my brother's cremated remains and his fingerprints brought all new kinds of emotions back onto the surface of my heart like I was starting the grieving process over again. I held my brother's ashes close to my heart, took a minute alone by myself, and cried. My mom received Jacob's actual copy of thumbprints and his hair, and she couldn't even look at it.

As she went through Jacob's clothes—she thought she was strong enough to go through them, but she wasn't close—she called me, crying. I told her that it was another sign that it just wasn't the right time yet. But then I realized my mom had found more drugs when she thought she had already cleaned everything, and that's what broke her. It brought trauma and terrible memories back into my mom's heart. It's something nobody else can understand unless you have lived through it yourself because, in reality, no one knew how big the struggle really was behind closed doors and what my mom and stepdad had to see and go through every day. I hurt for my mom, and it was opening more wounds for my mom. It felt impossible for her to get any type of grieving or healing for herself because every day felt like something new would happen. I sat on my step, reminding my mom over the phone that she was the one who had to see Jacob's room every day. She was the one who had to see that hallway and know that she would never see her son walk down it ever again. Hence, she needed to take whatever time she needed for herself. She needed to heal herself first before doing anything, and it wasn't anybody's damn business how they felt about it. I told her Jacob's cigarette smell scent on all his clothes would never be replaceable and just to know it was okay to take as long as she needed. If she needed ever to yell, scream, or cry as hard as she needed to, she could do it to me any time. At the right point in life and time, if there even is one for my mom, I told her she would have the right strength. She will feel when it's the right time and that Jacob will help her find that strength.

Days later, my mom received the call that it was time to pick up Jacob's belongings from the police station, another wound to reopen in my mom's heart. It was so unfair. So, instead of having my mom go through that horrible pain, my stepdad went and picked it up, and, again, this was another thing added to the grieving process. What people just didn't understand is that my mom and stepdad now had to see Jacob's belongings that he had on him during that time, the very last things my brother touched. It was terrible. You think something as simple as a toothbrush wouldn't hurt, but it's the worst feeling ever.

On May 5, my mom decided to start grief counseling. I was beyond proud of her for taking that huge step for her own mental health and stability. I knew

Jacob was right next to her to help guide her through challenging conversations with complete strangers. My mom texted me, telling me how horrible it was not realizing how many people in this world lose their children from an overdose, and she said it was terrible and overwhelming. Addiction is not supported nor talked about enough in life, and it's honestly ridiculous. So, two days later, I decided to do something in honor of my brother. I wanted to put Jacob's life and his story out to the public, to maybe help somebody out there struggling as well. I wanted people to know that having an addiction does not mean that you're a "bad person," like people made my brother out to be. We decided to get photos done with a photographer. To express how amazing Jacob was through our photos. Mom and I held a picture up of Jacob, cried and talked about all of Jacob's amazing accomplishments and how unique he was. I could feel in that room with the photographer that Jacob was in there also, and oddly enough, one of my brother's songs began playing across the radio. My mom and I cried and poured our hearts out as we took pictures expressing how unique Jacob really was, how much we love and miss him, and to educate the public more about overdose awareness and the lack of help in this world for addicts to receive the care and stability that rehabs severely lack. My mom and I will never stop advocating and speaking out until a change is made in the world. Addicts are suffering from a disease they didn't ask for or want.

Later that same day, we got back to my mom's house. She had me go through Jacob's clothes in his bedroom. When I was in his bedroom, goosebumps and chills ran through my body. I felt everything all at once, and I started crying with my mom when I glanced over and saw Jacob's belongings from the police station. His toothbrush, wallet, deodorant, shoes, and clothes were right in front of me, and it felt like a black demon reentering my mind. It brought me back to a very dark place in my head. When I saw Jacob's personal belongings, all I could think of was when my dad asked me one day, sitting outside of his house, "Who buys Jacob's things for him?"

I simply said, "Um, my mom."

My dad then said, "Well, she's a better person than me. He's a grown-ass man. I wouldn't be buying is deodorant and things for him."

I was beyond pissed off that day when he had the nerve to say that to me, and let me tell you this: my mom would do it a thousand more times for my brother if she were able to. It didn't matter what it was, she would provide *anything* for Jacob and me because that's what damn parents do for their children. I picked out clothes that reminded me the most of my brother, clothes that we had bought together from some of the best brother and sister bonding nights we ever had together. I got home, put on my brother's Carhartt, and stared at myself in the mirror. Tears were flowing down my face, hitting the sink counter. I didn't care. It was a flashback and a horrible image inside of my mind, like I could reverse time back and see Jacob wearing it as he would always be standing outside in front of the house by the bench smoking a cigarette, watching me pull into the driveway. When I would get out of the car, he would say to me, "Hey, there's my sissy." God, what I would do to hear that again one more time.

9

HONOR

As Mother's Day came this year, I didn't want to bother the hell out of my mom. I knew the day would be dreadful, so I just simply reminded her how amazing of a parent she indeed was and that Jacob missed her just as much as she missed him, that he loved her and would always continue to give her signs that he will forever watch over her. I know my brother knew how great our mom was. She is an absolutely incredible mom, and she will do anything literally for her children.

Having Jacob pass away has challenged my family's mental health in many ways. Still, all we can do is wake up every single day and try to find something positive about life. I know that Jacob is safe and hope-fully living the life he always deserved. I want to make my brother proud of me. I want him to see me get ev-erything I've always dreamed of. I struggle every day knowing my brother won't actually be present at my wedding or that he will never be able to hold my child one day. I struggle every time I hear one of Jacob's favorite songs playing through my car or hearing his voice and his contagious laugh playing over and over again when I can't sleep at night. It's on constant re-play. It doesn't just go away. It's a terrible demon I will always have, and I just have to face it and get through it mentally.

My mom is doing her damn best to honor and advocate for Jacob, making overdose awareness shirts, sending purple ribbons for any business or company she can get support from to wear purple in honor of my brother on August 31, which is Overdose Awareness Day. Jacob will forever be in our minds, our lives, and everything I do from now on. I know nothing will ever feel the same ever again, but I have to make the best out of life. My little brother has grown and matured so much through this. He has developed a huge passion for catfishing, and I think it brings him closer to Jacob. My mom and stepdad take Jacob with them wherever they go camping and leave a little bit of his ashes each time so that Jacob can fly and live his life anywhere he chooses to be. He is now spread over the mountains in North Carolina with my family, and a little more of Jacob is spread at his favorite fishing spot. We also have a piece of him in our vehicles to keep us safe and to watch over us every time we drive. We have ashes in our homes and nightstands as well.

Family dinner will never be the same, holidays or any family get-together because Jacob's beautiful smile will be missing. He was the jokester of the family, and he's gone and irreplaceable. Jacob was his own unique personality. I will never go to my mom's house again and feel complete because my other half isn't visible anymore. I will never hear "sissy" ever again, and I will look in the hallway every time and wait for him to come walking down it.

Some days are easier than other days when it comes to dark emotions and depression, but I try to stay positive. I hope and pray that Jacob is flying high and free and just beyond happy doing whatever he deserves to do every day. I know Jacob was broken, and he held onto anything that set him free. He felt like a lost cause in this life, but he wasn't to us at all, and I just pray every night before I go to sleep that he is so happy and loving who he truly is in heaven—the Jacob we always saw, but he couldn't see it himself.

As a family, we decided that every year for Jacob's birthday we will all do something special together in honor of him, to celebrate how amazing Jacob really was, how much we miss and love him, and cherish the wonderful years we were able to have with him. Throughout these horrible months, I had one person who was incredible to me named Miranda. She never stopped messaging me, sending me positive words and guidance to help me through tough struggles and darkness. She had helped my mom multiple times through the years when my mom came to her for questions and support when Jacob was still with us. She has been beyond great to my family, and I know she loved Jacob so much. She has checked on me every week since Jacob has passed, just to check up on me making sure I'm doing okay. She has let me go off about strong emotions I have felt. I just let it all out to her, and she comes back saying she's so proud of me being honest about a lot of things. She is the only friend who has checked on me numerous times and continues to check in. Even if I don't say anything back, she says she understands and to just take care of myself. For that, I am so grateful for her and blessed to have someone care about me like that in life.

With Jacob being gone, my perspective towards life has changed tremendously. Life has taught me that time and life itself are so precious, not to take anything for granted, and to not waste time on the smallest petty things that aren't going to matter days later. Be positive about life, treat people well, and enjoy every small moment. When you see others struggling, please help, guide, and support them, and stop judging so much. When people like my brother struggle, they really need a lot of love and support, and they don't need things like money. All they want is for someone to tell them, "Hey, I'm here for you." I will never forget sitting on my mom's pool deck one summer day with Jacob. I looked at him, and I said, "Jacob, why are you doing this to yourself?"

He looked at me and said, "Sis, you'll never understand. You think I want to be an addict every day? Hell no, I don't want to be an addict. I want a good life and to be healthy again, but I wake up every damn day, and it feels like a thousand bugs are crawling through my skin until I get something. It hurts, and it's the worst feeling, so I just fix it quickly." "Plus, when you get told time after time again that you're a nobody in life and a junkie from so many people, you start believing that about yourself sis." I told him, "Jacob, you are so much more than that. You are so amazing and who cares what the hell people think about you, prove them all wrong." He replied, "I do Selena, I just want people to accept me in life, and they don't. I can't get our own damn dad to accept me as his son." That exact day I changed because I didn't know how my brother felt inside, but I knew it was my job to make sure he knew how much I loved him and that I would always be there to support him and if he needed anything from me, he knew I would do it. Sadly, there weren't enough people to say that to my brother. Having an addiction does not mean you're a bad person; you're sick, and it's a true disease that takes over your brain and body, so don't ever sit there and think that if they want to stop, they could so easily or that they chose that lifestyle. That's not true at all. Addiction is a true disease, and if you're not educated enough about it, I suggest you not judge an addict struggling because addicts struggle with mental health issues on top of everything. Depression also plays a huge factor in all of it. When you're depressed, nothing can change the way you feel inside—nobody's words, no counseling, nothing. And there are insufficient resources to help with addiction. Rehabs and other places want to medicate. Medicating someone quickly is not okay all the time, especially when addiction is already in their health records, but sadly places do not see it like that. Addiction is not talked about nor supported enough, and at some point, people must stop judging and stand up and rise together to make a change in this world. It's so sad that this world can talk about so many other topics that really aren't as important as addiction and mental health issues.

Still, when it comes to the word "addiction," people judge addicts so fast and look at addicts like scum. It's unfortunate and disgusting. Also, we must stop looking at drug dealers like good people and helping them make a living and profit off of selling poison to innocent people and killing so many individuals. Drug dealers know that people will keep coming back for more drugs. A dealer doesn't give a shit about what they are selling you; it's not their problem what happens to you, and that's disgusting.

My mom and I just won't stop talking and educating about overdose awareness, and it needs to get supported so much more. She and I are naloxone certified, and we carry naloxone on us all the time. Knowing the signs of someone overdosing is so important. This is because I know many people do not know the difference between seeing someone in a parking lot sleeping in their vehicle versus overdosing in that vehicle. Naloxone can save somebody's life in a terrible moment, so I wish more people would take overdose more seriously and carry it on them as well. If you have never seen someone overdosed, be thankful. It's the worst image you will ever see in your life, and that image will never go away, especially when it's your own brother. Also, always remember this: every single person is addicted to something—everyone. It doesn't matter if it's something like coffee, food, or soda, but your brain triggers you to think that you must have that certain obsession every day, and that's exactly the same way an addict feels.

I have learned that nobody is perfect. No one. But my brother was a good-ass person. My brother loved and respected anyone who treated him the exact same way. My brother stood up for his family. Jacob was loyal, always had manners, smiled, and always seemed happy, even if he wasn't okay inside. He always treated me so well and never treated me any differently through the years of struggling.

For the people who judged my family, but more importantly, my brother, shame on you. But I've learned to shrug it off, because my family and I know how amazing Jacob was. We know who was actually present in Jacob's life and who wasn't. The opinions and judgments will never change, as I just heard recently screamed at my face that my brother was a "junkie." That's okay, go ahead and say that, because what you say about my brother doesn't matter. My brother was not a damn junkie, and karma will come around to you. As every person has their own faults, I have learned people point fingers and judge others because they don't want to look at their own problems. It's always easier to overlook yourself. That's okay, because truth always comes out eventually. I know I am doing what I need to do, and that's telling the truth about my brother, supporting him, and educating people on the truth.

My family and I stuck by Jacob. We never gave up faith. I've realized that if you couldn't experience how incredible my brother was, you missed out on knowing and having a great relationship with a one-of-a-kind person because Jacob was so great. My family and I will hopefully grow stronger together from Jacob. I hope our family doesn't fall backwards or sink down into a dark place, instead we need to honor Jacob's life forever. To ensure Jacob never goes unknown throughout life and our future moving ahead. Nothing will ever be the same, but we must live in memory of him. But, I promise you, I will never allow someone who is uneducated about addiction talk about my brother, acting like they knew him and knew what our family went through. I will never let Jacob's spirit be broken. To be completely honest, I'm lucky enough that I'm not a damn addict because it can happen to anybody. So stop thinking you are any better than the next person standing behind you. It's just very unfortunate that my beautiful brother was addicted to something so deadly.

But, Jacob was so much more than what people saw him out to be in the end. I'm tired of people saying at the end that Jacob was an addict and that's all there was about him. Jacob was his own person, an individual who was so unique in his own incredible ways. Truly, my brother never looked sick and he shinned anywhere he was. He lit up any room with his goofy laugh and always wanted to have a great time. Jacob taught me to never live life too seriously. Laugh, joke and have fun doing the smallest things, even if it was hanging out around the house making a new recipe we found online together in the kitchen. Every single-family dinner or event will be incomplete without Jacob's presence. We will never feel complete ever again, but we can make sure Jacob is honored forever. As his sister, I will live and become a better version of myself for Jacob.

Still, I will tell you the most important thing. I've come to peace with knowing nobody can ever sell my brother that black poison again. Those dealers cannot reach my brother in heaven. He is free.

Always remind yourself one thing: if you cannot understand why a person is grieving so long about a loss, consider yourself fortunate that you do not understand it. If you have never seen someone struggle with addiction, watching someone die slowly, withdrawing, shaking so badly, and watching life through their hurt eyes, be beyond thankful and grateful. It is the worst damn thing you will ever see and an image that becomes a forever nightmare that you live with and can't get away from because every single time you close your eyes to sleep at night, your brain reminds you what happened. I will forever ask myself one question: why my brother?

***

To my brother Jacob,

Time, brother. There's never enough time. To say I loved you is an understatement. Jacob, you were my only full-blood sibling. The bond you and I had together is unreplaceable and so strong, and I knew no one could ever break us apart. You were always there for me, through anything good or bad. You saved me through so many reckless nights being young and crazy, picking me up, fighting for me, always supporting me, and cheering me on to achieve anything I ever worked towards in my life and wanted for my future. I love you more than anything else in this world.

I always looked up to you, and I wanted to do anything you did growing up. I was always so damn proud of you. You were so full of life. We wrestled around in the living room and watched WWE growing up, and we would pretend we were jumping from the ropes onto Mom's bed. We had our certain shows we watched together, whipped ass playing video games, aced every level in *Guitar Hero*, joked around, and did so many hilarious pranks to our siblings. We would laugh our asses off even if we knew we were going to get into trouble. Watching you play sports made me so proud to sit there as your little sister to support and cheer you on every time. I was so proud to let anyone know that you were my brother. Every single baseball practice, game, wrestling match, or tournament, I sat there, proud that we were the Williams kids. We would throw a *W* up with our fingers, and I cheered my ass off every time you were up to bat or walking to the middle of the mat.

I always prayed for you every night before going to bed that you would prove all these people who screwed you over in life wrong. I wanted you to prove to people that you were going to overcome this terrible disease. I wanted to see you get everything you ever wanted in life because you deserved it, brother. Every car ride together jamming to music, going to Arby's all the time to grub out, every party or even every time playing cornhole, being my beer pong partner, having a fire and drinks at night, and hitting golf balls with the bat as hard so we could see in the fields I will cherish forever. You always wanted to clean my car because you always thought it was dirty, which are moments I will never get again. I will miss arguing about our Phillies and NFL, getting a football betting card, and having Sunday football days at Dad's house eating chili and dips. It will never feel the same to me ever again, and my happiness towards watching sports honestly will fade a little each year it comes because I will not have you next to me watching the game, telling me that your team is better than mine.

Fishing now, I am honored to have your fishing pole to use every time I fish. It will make me feel closer to you and help me feel like you're always right there fishing beside me. I am beyond blessed and thankful you were my older brother. I am blessed for every single fishing trip, night fishing, bullshitting around as rascal teenagers getting into harmless trouble together, and every Fireball shot or Bud Light we shared. Every shark fishing trip to the beach, throwing the football on the beach, and just enjoying those summer days, I will always remember.

You taught me so much in life, Jacob, and I am honored to be your sister. A lot of who I am today is because of you. I will remember every single memory together and hold them so close to my heart, and I promise to you, I will tell my future children about how amazing their Uncle Jacob was. I hope my future kids are so athletic, smart, and funny just like you, and

I hope they love to fish just as much as you did. I will talk up to you in the sky every single night.

Please help guide me throughout life and the struggles I may face in the future. Watch over the family, but mostly Mom and Dad always. Continue to please send Mom signs and remind her that you can love and miss her as much as you can. Take care of yourself, Jacob. Have fun with your friends and family in heaven with you. Love yourself—love every bit of who you are, and I hope you see what we always saw in you, an amazing and incredible man. You are no longer in pain, and you are never going to suffer again, brother. Do whatever makes you happy. Be so happy every single day and fly high, beautiful angel.

I will see you again one day in heaven. I love you with all my heart, Jacob, and thank you for being the best big brother. I will forever miss you and wonder what you are doing. Just remember to always take care of yourself; you are so amazing, Jacob, and you live the life you always deserved. No one can ever hurt you again. You are safe and free, my angel. I love you with all my heart, brother, and like you said to me the very last time we ever talked to each other, "I'll talk to you soon, okay?"

I love you forever, Jacob.

Your Sissy

9 781638 378389